POP-UP SHRINES

poems by

Linda Drach

Finishing Line Press
Georgetown, Kentucky

POP-UP SHRINES

for Jack

ACKNOWLEDGMENTS

Thanks are due to the editors of these journals for publishing the following
poems, sometimes in an earlier version:

CALYX: "At the Appointed Time"
Cathexis Northwest: "You Must Be a Saint"
Clackamas Literary Review: "Shoehorned"
Crab Creek Review: "Practice" and "Treasures"
Sweet: "Closed Doors," "Trapdoors," and "Cosmic Doors"
The Examined Life: "Hysterical Strength"
Verseweavers: "Every Day I Get Closer to Knowing How to Say Goodbye,"
"Still Life," and "Three Days on Cloud Mountain"
The Write Launch: "Why Our Marriage Works" and "The Widow Sifts
through the Rubble"

Publisher: Leah Huete de Maines
Editor: Christen Kincaid
Cover Art: Linda Drach
Author Photo: Susan Montgomery
Cover Design: Elizabeth Maines McCleavy

Order online: www.finishinglinepress.com
also available on amazon.com

Author inquiries and mail orders:
Finishing Line Press
PO Box 1626
Georgetown, Kentucky 40324
USA

Contents

PROLOGUE: LETTER TO MY BELOVED

Dearest—

You like to say *I don't deserve you*, as acknowledgment of what I have done for you over the past eight years during your physical decline, and what you expect I will do for you in the future. It is a sincere expression of deep love and appreciation, as well as a demonstration of your need for reassurance. I suspect you want me to say what I usually say: *that's ridiculous*. Or: *come on, we're in this together*. What would happen if I really stopped to evaluate how much each of deserves?

Thinking about our relationship in transactional terms feels unkind and unsavory. Relationships are not jobs. People are not assets or liabilities. Can we define what makes us want to give love—or withhold it? Who is the arbiter of how much love is worth? Words matter. Yours make me wonder: how much do I deserve and should I have demanded more? The questions are uncomfortable. I'd rather be a failed saint than a fool.

I am faced with a conundrum because I am trying to be more honest with myself in every way, and this authentic inquiry must, of course, extend to our long and fundamental relationship. So, when you say you do not deserve me, I need to consider your statement objectively. Please consider the following:

INVOICE FOR CAREGIVING SERVICES

1.   **Meals**—It's true I used to make homemade risotto and dolmas, whereas our usual dinner now is steamed broccoli and Trader Joe's kim bap—but still, I plan, purchase, prepare, serve, and clean up an estimated 900 meals per year. Annual birthday cakes, your favorite pickled carrots, and Thanksgiving turkeys provided on an in-kind basis. **$540,000**
2.   **Laundry**—Daily loads of clothing. Sheets once/week. No ironing. **$312,000**

3.   Housekeeping, All Other—Everything else needed to run a household; examples provided are illustrative, and far from exhaustive. Scrubbing floors. Paying bills. Cleaning the dog's ears. Vacuuming. Creating a safe and serene home with soul. **$624,000**

4.   Companionship—Nightly Netflix when I would rather be reading or writing or kickboxing at the gym, but I want to spend time with you, and I know you feel safer when I'm sitting next to you in the dark. **$436,800**

5.   Medical Case Management—Tracking, scheduling, and attending medical appointments. Interpreting results. Managing your prescriptions. Diagnosing your first heart condition when your doctors missed it. **$312,000**

6.   Impacts on Caregiver Health—I gained 30 pounds. My cholesterol doubled. Even my feet grew a size, which means I no longer fit into my chestnut brown Frye Campus 12R leather boots, and now they cost $500/pair, an outrageous sum. **$500,500**

7.   The Great Funk of 2022—That year, you gave up entirely. You seemed to enjoy being mean to me. In December, I cried every day except Christmas. **$2 million**

8.   Loss of Use—The cost of renting a replacement while the original is being repaired, usually awarded when a person is no longer able to enjoy an asset due to damage caused by someone else's negligence. Did you take the best care of yourself when you had the chance? I no longer have a partner who can fully participate in life with me. There is no replacement for you, and I miss you. **$10 million**

9.   Opportunity Costs—Everything I could have done, but didn't, because I was caring for you. Itemized report available upon request. **$20 million**

BALANCE DUE: $34,725,300

You will rightly say there are credits that should be applied to this account. Because I spent so much time at home, I started writing, fulfilling a lifelong dream. Under other circumstances, I might not have deepened my friendships or adopted a puppy or changed jobs in order to cultivate better work-life balance. These things matter, but the more additions and subtractions I make, the more I can see this quantitative assessment does not answer the original question, which is whether you deserve me. It only shows that you cannot afford me.

Here is a fact, however, that might make an objective observer conclude that you are not worthy of my $35 million investment. At times, your suffering made you depressed, which caused you to become insular and selfish. Maybe this is an unavoidable consequence of chronic illness and unmitigated pain. Maybe this is not your fault. Still, I didn't abandon you, even though you abandoned yourself, and by extension, me. So, the question I must consider next is this: if you do not deserve me, and if I will not or cannot leave you, what might help balance our accounts?

For starters, and I know you'll hate this, I want to write about this—my feelings, our experience. I want the freedom to say and share whatever I want.

BLUE EDEN

The bluebells are wild now, choking
our rows of spinach and peas. Look at them
crowding the daffodils. I didn't plant them.
I don't accept them. I crouch in the dirt,
jagged knife raised. Stab at the earth,
rooting out clumps. I see the threat clearly.
This bed we made—it's being invaded.

Do bluebells seem weak? They wilt
when picked, but try to remove them.
The bulbs are entrenched like grudges.
He sits by the window, watching me dig.
His young wife—OK, middle aged.
But he likes my legs. Says the little spider
veins are as hot as lace stockings.

If I dig deep enough, maybe I'll remember
how we coaxed beauty from meager beginnings.
Four strong hands. Plucked blossoms
he arranged like a crown in my hair.
He hasn't laughed for years. How long
will I kneel on this carpet of grief?
The bluebells are unruly.

I don't know if I can live here.

WHY OUR MARRIAGE WORKS

You sing songs to the pug in your fake Cantonese
and seem surprised when he doesn't understand. You make coffee
a party: gleaming French presses and hand-thrown mugs
plucked from thrift store shelves. Unpretentious
about fashion, you covet coats like a boy who grew up
always cold. Because once, you gave your good wool coat
to a man in a flop house called the Snake Ranch. You rescue
hummingbird nests blown out of trees and see sculpture
in piles of rubble. Because you love, with equal zeal, begonias
and babies and sheetrock screws. Because you love the world
more than you hate the world. You dislike Christmas
but still twist twigs into wreaths with me. Because everything
you touch—rock or metal or leather or wood—
you shape into beauty. Because you did that
to me. Because we decorate our home with opaque stones
balanced on brass nozzles, and bowls of balled wool, and curly
willow branches hung with blue feathers—pop-up shrines
we build from common objects and we live our life
among them stunned and blessed.

STILL LIFE
(death rattle #1)

Of all the paintings he made in his life,
the round-bottomed pears, the Chinese lantern pods
artfully crouched around bottles of wine,
only a few remain, and the studio has grown dusty.
He could go in there if he wanted, pick up
a brush with arthritic fingers, imagine
a fresh place to start.

He may still read *War & Peace*
or drive the six hours to visit his brother
or perfect his barbequed ribs.
He might learn to use Bluesky
or just lie down and play every one of his Dylan albums
in chronological order, listening to *Blonde on Blonde* twice.

But the light is waning. The maples are turning to scarlet
and caramel.

Winter advances.

He might paint her an apple that looks so real,
she'll fill her mouth with dry canvas.

ENOUGH

The dollars compounding in digital vaults have waited long enough.

I say it's time to admit there will be no plein air classes
in Tuscany. No Grand Canyon skydives. Not even another coffee
at our favorite lakeside cabin—the one only reached by row boat,
where herons pose for sunrise on sewing needle legs.

It's time to embrace a different kind of travel. For you,
a Grade A wheelchair with jazzy saddlebags to hold field guides
and binoculars and maybe a handful of fat joints and matches.
For me, a tower of books—stand-ins for the stacked aspirations

that teetered, and swayed, and spilled across the floor.
I'm done saving for Someday. Let's invest
in local markets: handmade velvet quilts and sea salt macarons.
Tulips and crab cakes and saffron ice cream cones.

Naysayers warn you can never save enough, but I say they're wrong.
This is our wealth. Exploring the world together—
right here, in this small house—
linen sketch books, Italian pasta, a jungle of houseplants, harmonicas.

CLOSED DOORS

My husband spent forty years crawling through the bellies of ships and lugging chainsaws up ladders and stacking boulders on top of one another, so now he can't move without a walker and a lot of pain. He spends most of his days in his power lift recliner, napping or watching TV shows about men doing things he can't do. Sometimes, the shows feature men searching for something special or uncanny—like Aztec gold or Bigfoot—but often, the activities are more prosaic. Men rebuilding car engines. Men remodeling cabins. Men repairing watches. Men milking cows. Once, I found him watching a You Tube video about men fabricating a gutter and installing it on a garage. Sometimes, he tells me stories about these guys over dinner, as if they were his friends from work. He doesn't watch those shows with me. We watch 'Gardeners' World' or 'Chef's Table' or You Tube videos of people walking through the Tate Modern. Our favorite show right now is 'Somebody Somewhere,' which follows a group of friends in small-town Kansas, as they experience shimmering moments of vulnerability and connection while eating French toast, taking singing lessons, and standing in corn fields. Sometimes, I talk about these Kansas friends at dinner, saying something like, *it's such a gift to watch grace unfolding.* My husband says nothing. He stares at his plate, adding salt and smoked paprika to whatever I've put on it.

THREE DAYS ON CLOUD MOUNTAIN

Before sunrise, we arrange ourselves
cross-legged on floor cushions or perched
on wooden stools, our legs bent back
and tucked under. We are here to practice
simple things. Sitting. Breathing. And later,
walking. Rain thrums the roof and drips
off the gutters. Closer, the soft susurrus
of breath lulls us like a tranquil ocean.
In and out. On and on. Until the brass
singing bowl hums 1, 2, 3—

and we slowly transition onto mossy paths
tossed with yellow leaves. We walk
single file, black umbrellas held high.
We walk towards nothing. We walk
to feel stones beneath the soles of our feet.
To feel the gentle wobble of proprioception.
Back home, illness stalks my husband
the way the cougar that owns these woods
may be tracking us now, as we practice
silent attention, becoming better company
to what we fear.

Tomorrow, when I return to ticking clocks
and heartbreak and my sticky attachment
to the way things used to be, will I
remember how to watch my thoughts
release and drop, like these maple leaves
that fall in graceful, desultory spirals?
I hope I can remember. It's my choice.
I could be anything.

An open umbrella. A leaf, letting go.

LOVE POEM OVERSHADOWED BY ROTTING CORPSE
(death rattle #2)

I meant to fill your life with all you deserve.
Sun-warmed peaches drizzled with honey.
A name for every bird. I swore you'd never
be sorry. Now, I say: *I know I don't show it,*
but I really do love you. You see how I am?
Always telling on myself. I open my mouth
and worms fall out. Why can't I just say
I love you?

It's the unburied dead in my head, my love.
A childhood alone in my dad's dark truck,
tavern doors swinging. The little bag of peanuts
and Coke long gone. Salty-sweet dreams,
watching the cars. Everyone else going home
to someone warm like you.

FUCHSIA SATURDAY
(death rattle #3)

Here's a partial list of things I can't do anymore: drive a car, pull on socks, reach a box on a high shelf, buy what I want at the hardware store. Today is the annual sale at our local Garden Center. Ten dollars for a dozen fuchsias, the shade-loving blooms that droop. My wife will bring home armloads. When I'm not in too much pain, I stoke my old dreams of building a workshop. I gaze out windows. Scribble on paper napkins. Yak at the wife about J bolts and sill plates. I see the life I want so clearly. Building birdhouses and bookshelves and maybe even a wooden boat beneath three sets of soaring scissor trusses. But when I'm in too much pain, I hunt for my gun, which my wife has hidden. Yesterday, she found something dead in the yard. The body had been rotting in place for weeks. Fur picked clean. A rat, squirrel, or opossum that's now just meat. I didn't see it, but she brought me a picture on her phone. More things I can't do: walk six steps to the garden, kneel to plant Spring flowers, scrape up and dispose of dead vermin. Without my fat plans, I don't recognize myself. I studied the picture. Not much left of the face. Maybe a whisker. A stringy tail thick as my pinkie. Was the end a quick strike? I want a lightning of wings, but platinum wires and cunning gears wind my fitful heart—like it or not. Prolonging the decay. On days like today, I beg my wife for bullets. She brings me pink blossoms.

THE WEIGHT

Before he got sick, he showered me in metal. Elaborate tin combs for my copper-colored hair. A beloved bacon fork. A whimsical chicken he pieced to life from soup cans. And I gifted him with Crêpes Suzette. My grandmother's pierogi. All kinds of jam. Blackberry. Blueberry. Raspberry. Peach. Summer's intensity captured in glass. Our home overflowed with oddly specific tokens of affection. Now, we share appointments and test results and cracker crumbs on T-shirts in front of the TV. My love wraps his arms around me, and whispers in my ear, *I don't want to be a burden.* He's heavy as a sack. He tells me to slow down. I can't slow down. I don't want to slow down. If I slow down, I'll probably drink through a case of wine. Summer's intensity captured in glass. If I slow down—if I set the load down—what will happen to all this beauty?

HYSTERICAL STRENGTH

This winter feels relentless. I want time alone
in a seaside hotel. Coffee in bed. A stack of books.
Long walks without looking at the clock. Instead,
we have snowstorms and days without power
and it seems like you had another little stroke. Our home
is 33 degrees. I load the Jeep with your walker and pills.
Your favorite slippers. The big foam wedges you need
to sleep. A cooler of food. Blankets. Pillows. Icy Hot.
Ice packs. Where's the ice scraper? I scrape the windshield
with a tin of mints. We two-step slick sidewalks
into the car—there's one room left at the Motel 6
and it's ours, as long as we can get there. You're confused
and sage, like you get when a circuit pops in your brain.
You look at me and say, *when the storm finally ends,*
our house will sing, but I won't be there to hear it.

I'm your light and heat, and I feel so tired.
Kind people tell me the stupidest things. *You can't run*
on empty. You need to recharge. Safe in the motel,
I heat oatmeal, check email, and help you cope
with the desk chair with wheels. I call PGE, decode
the TV, and message your doctor. Each day,
I watch you flicker and fade. We live like candles
burned down to the wicks. This is no vacation,
but it's not a crisis yet. When we need it
the most, I hope I can be like those women
you read about sometimes, the ones who lift cars
to save the kids pinned beneath. I hope I have it in me.
A surge so strong I forget how much it hurts.

IF I COULD HARVEST MY TEARS, I'D SELL THEM TO BUY MORE ROSÉ

A worried friend gives me a jar of lavender-mint sea salt
in exchange for a promise to take care of myself. I honor
my commitments. Is that why I am drinking wine
and crying in my bathtub?

The bath provides a break from caring for my husband, who is ill
and depressed, and who yells instead of crying—too bad
because crying rinses the body of stress hormones.
I'd like to tell him

about the British company that sells table salt
made from human tears. Sadness, anger, envy, and boredom—
they all taste different. Back when we visited museums
and gardens and people who don't live on Netflix,

I might have been surprised to learn there are so many
kinds of tears. That was when he knew my secrets
and asked about my day. Before I understood how a woman
with graduate degrees and credit cards and a silver key

in her open palm could look at a locked door and feel nothing
but stuck. Tonight, my tears taste bitter and complex,
with hints of bruised apple and smoke from a Barbie
with her hair on fire. It's revolting, of course—

but part of me must savor the old, familiar flavor.
My friend is half-right. A hot bath *is* relaxing. But look
at my skin—the angry shock of pink. If I knew how
to take care of myself, I'd have gotten out by now.

YOU MUST BE A SAINT

That's what they say, the friends who hear him bark
when I leave for the gym or buy the wrong soap,

the ones who glimpse the shit stains, who balk
at the thought of so much toenail trimming.

But how can they know? Martyrdom
is not my calling. It's just a sticky vat I fell into.

My beloved is dying—and I fret
about my fat and fuss over the dusting.

My suffering beloved says he wants to kill himself
and then we bicker about dinner.

Yes, each disagreement starts with skillful, textbook framing:
When you said [X], I felt [Y] because I need to feel [Z].

But things devolve quickly. He yells, *I know—but I'm dying!*
I know! I shout back. *But you don't have to be such a dick about it.*

I keep a rat on a leash in my chest. Tethered like a vacuum,
it lives on crumbs. It gobbles them up with waxy tongue.

No one knows. No one hears me crying hard in the car,
radio loud to crowd out my pleas: *oh God, oh God,*

how can I ever be forgiven for forgetting to love—
for wasting the time we have left?

LOVE POEM WITH CODEPENDENT TENDENCIES AND SIGNS OF SPRING

Look out the window, love. See the crocus bursting from their hugs of mud? You stare at the TV, pill bottles at your elbow. Bombs, fires, and flooding. *See the sparrows nesting in the eaves of the porch?* You curl in on yourself like a fist. As a child, I tip-toed through yawning days draped in clean white sheets, unable to feel happier than the least happy person in the household. But see the daffodils? They can't keep their sunny heads bent. My body shows signs of discontent. I try to ignore them. Shoulders holding doorknobs. A forehead that throbs like a bell being pressed. I love you. You suffer. I can't save you. We descend through musty passages that narrow like funnels and just when I feel I have lost myself, I discover new rooms. Silent ballrooms gilded in leaves. An oak-paneled den full of bones and teeth. I can't help it. The world keeps finding ways to delight me. I wish I could share it with you. The purple hyacinth. The dark corners feathered in wonder. My words are paper birds that fly away.

DECONSTRUCTION

For three wet decades, your beloved
laid a thousand bricks a day. Now, his body
falls apart like a house riddled with rot.

You prop him up,
but all you want to do
is write. You live two lives.

As *caregiver/wife*, you're required
to be nice. No anger or unrest,
lest you undermine him.

If you forget, a gesture reminds you.
His palm. Pushing down. Unsaid,
but signified: *Keep a lid on it, kitten.*

When it happens, you repress
but *your writer* will express it.
Your writer isn't nice.

Words are like bricks.
You are building the foundation
to a house you can live in.

You build yourself back with black ink.

INVISIBLE INK

All at once, my pens are running out of ink. The black pens, the blue pens, even the red pens—all my favorites, which are nothing fancy. I prefer plastic ballpoints with matching caps that come ten to a package. Now, I'm even working my way through the giveaways and stowaways from Indian restaurants, mortgage companies, coastal hotels, florists, hairdressers, and credit unions. Now, I'm forced to scavenge through junk drawers and old backpacks to find one that works. Who am I without a pen? I've spent many waking hours with a pen stuck behind my right ear, a gesture so signature my tiny toddler niece imitated me with glee thirty years ago, using only a pen, and we all understood the joke. My husband, a builder and artist, draws out ideas for inventions; he tries to express himself through pictures. I write myself notes, so I can hold on to life's beautiful ephemera. On the back of an electric bill: *Even the Dumpster is dripping with Christmas lights.* On a gum wrapper: *Overheard on Burnside, "Fuck you and give me a hug."* Memory is written in invisible ink. It's unreliable. Plus, the hand that holds a pen can't clutch a cocktail or a cookie or a pill. The hand that holds a pen feels like it's being held back.

TRAPDOORS

I've heard people with perfectionistic tendencies, like me, often develop secret habits that help us escape from the pressure of constantly failing to meet our own expectations. These trapdoors lead to private spaces where we can rest. I have a trapdoor, and the space beneath it feels like a warm bath or a seat at the table in my grandmother's kitchen. I'm always welcome there. It doesn't matter if I'm dressed to the nines or wearing flannel pajamas and a sweat-stained hoodie. The trapdoor says come as you are. Beneath the trap door, my harsh thoughts soften like balls of wool. I knit them into a provisional self-acceptance that hugs me like a cashmere sweater. I love my trapdoor. I love my safe velvet box. Does this seem extreme? Every castle has a secret room. So does every haunted house. Trapdoors are common on cargo ships and in magic acts; they are an essential feature of the gallows. Like me, trapdoors are efficient. The Holy Roman Emperor, another enlightened despot, mandated the use of trapdoors in reusable coffins. Every day, I expertly navigate spreadsheets and sickness and endless spools of news delivering autocrats and children with limbs blown off. I like knowing there's a quick exit if I need it. Sadly, climbing back out has gotten too hard, so I had to make a change. I know it's still there, but I don't use it anymore. In other words, I stopped drinking.

COSMIC DOORS

Now that my husband can't drive, I'm responsible for the car—pumping gas, putting air in the tires, all the preventive maintenance. I dislike instant oil changes the most because I'm afraid of driving into the pit. This afternoon, Billy and Manuel greet me as I pull my Subaru into Valvoline. Manuel snaps on a long pair of black rubber gloves, while Billy yells, *Show Time!* Manuel guides me into Bay 1, indicating with stiff rubber-clad thumbs the proper way to angle my tires. His expression is bored. My husband tells me he is visited by angels in his dreams, eight-foot shadowy beings. He says their presence is reassuring; it envelops him in love. Maybe that's why he sleeps so much. Some days, I can barely wake him for meals or to say goodbye when I leave for my day's activities. Our cosmic relatives are showing him how to navigate non-linear time. They don't need to multitask. They don't care about grocery shopping or gym classes or oil changes. They don't care about billing cycles or menopause or sell-by dates. When I was younger, I dreamed about walking through fields of sunflowers. Now, in the liminal space of my parked car, waiting for Billy and Manuel to finish draining and replacing my fluids, I fill out my advance directive. Comfort, please. No heroic measures. Suspended over the pit, I think about hypothetical doors and choose which one I want to walk through.

LOVE POEM WITH EXISTENTIAL CRISIS
(death rattle #4)

We had a great love story, so I thought my life would never lack direction. Simple cause and effect. Then illness spun me onto circuitous paths. Latinate answers and tepid predictions. Bloodless rooms. Crickets swarming—or maybe those were nurses, in crisp green gowns. I misplaced my aspirations. My standard answer when asked about tomorrow: *Assuming I wake up, I'll stumble around on my painful stumps and try to be cheerful. And you?* I listened to one of your guided meditations. A woman said, *we are most ourselves when we are lost.* A horrifying thought. It means I am a shallow bowl, trying to hold floods. I am nothing, cantilevered over nothing. I am a trapdoor through which I keep falling. Doctors can't get me back on track. They send questionnaires, wanting to know if I feel more like a razor blade or a potato. They ask me to keep a mood journal. What is the mood called when your life feels like a turned-out pocket? I keep these details to myself. Maybe whisper them to the stoic monitor that blinks all night, watching my broken heart beat. But you're still beside me. Like otters, we hold hands as we sleep. To keep me from floating away from you in the dark.

DEATH, I'VE GROWN TIRED OF GAZING INTO THE GLOBES OF YOUR EYES
(death rattle #5)

A mountain lion attacked a group of cyclists
on a forest trail nearby.

It picked off the oldest. The one who lagged behind.
The newspapers say the victim was lucky

because her friends fought back. Even pried the lion's jaws
from the woman's mangled face.

I tell you this calmly. After years of nightly stand-offs, Death,
I know what you like. Which details will excite you.

How your shoulder muscles twitch
at the conjured pleasure of teeth crunching bone.

I shift my limbs painfully under the quilt.
Close my eyes. Play dead.

Part of me hoping you'll yawn and slink away.
Part of me hoping you'll pounce while we're alone.

SYMBIOSIS

(n) the close relationship between two organisms. Symbiosis can be beneficial, neutral, or harmful to one or both organisms. Symbiotic relationships are a driving force of evolution.

I.   **Mutualism**. We did everything together. We were the kind of couple that made people sigh with envy or want to throw up. We didn't care what other people thought. We loved being together. We loved listening to live chamber music and bluegrass and jazz. We loved to scour thrift stores and eat at Burmese restaurants. We got certified as Master Gardeners. We bought a canoe. We explored unshared interests without complaint. He tried yoga. I learned to mix mortar and lay brick. Even everyday chores provided opportunities to grow closer. He washed the dishes; I dried. I folded the clothes; he ironed. We often showered together, so we could keep talking and laughing while getting ready for the day. The word inseparable comes to mind. Maybe it was because we were not young when we found each other. I was 30; he was 50. That seems young now. But the age difference made us both aware, from the very beginning, that our relationship clock was ticking. Each day that passed was one day less we had to spend together. One day less to benefit from what the other offered. My vitality. His creativity. His strength. My common sense. I was the head; he was the heart. Why equivocate? Why not be all-in? We each seemed better together.

II.   **Commensalism**. I have an actuarial mindset, so I always understood the probability of being left alone. But I didn't expect to be alone while we were still together. As it turns out, I was young—younger than I realized. Too young to know how easily a bright life can be engulfed by a fungus. At first, his changes were hardly noticeable—low energy, irritation, confusion. I noticed. He wasn't himself. He didn't want to go to concerts. He didn't want to have dinner with friends. He was tired. Couldn't I see that? I saw it. His doctor didn't, so I researched his symptoms and sent the doctor annotated articles from the *New England Journal of*

Medicine. I requested tests, which yielded diagnoses. There were surgeries and pills and more pills and more surgeries. There was less thrifting and gardening, less convivial dishwashing. We sold the canoe. Pain overwhelmed him. He withdrew from life—and from me—spending more and more time in front of the TV. Before there was an 'us,' I liked reading and writing and taking long walks. I attended silent meditation retreats. I knew how to be alone, and truly enjoyed it. I was just out of practice. One September afternoon, I watched a leaf dangle and spin by a slim, silvery thread, and I thought: maybe this transition time is a kindness. I'm learning how to live without him.

III. **Parasitism.** And then, she was no longer young. He depended on her to provide his basic needs, and his suffering erased what they were. It was shocking, but it shouldn't have surprised her. Forty percent of known life forms survive by feeding on a host. Ticks, mites, fleas, lice, tapeworms, roundworms, hookworms, flukes. None of these are A-list housemates, but they know how to stay alive. Humans appropriated the word leech to mean a hanger-on who takes advantage of another. But, remember, the leech will die without the host's blood. The leech is in a life and death situation. There is short-term suffering for the host—leech bites can cause red blotches or itchy rashes, swelling around the lips and eyes, fainting, dizziness, and difficulty breathing—but the leech falls off when its needs are satisfied. It's only life and death for the host if there's an internal attachment. *OK*, she though*t, there's the answer*: she just couldn't let him get under her skin. During this period, she closed parts of herself off. She shut down so much she no longer thought of herself as an 'I.' She asked herself, and found no answer, *how much can something change before it becomes something else?*

IV. **Commensalism.** One good thing about growing older is understanding that everything is always changing, and everything looks different when viewed through a wide lens. Even leeches. Up close, they are revolting. But leeches have been used for at least 2,500 years—in short-term bursts—to heal disease and restore balance in their hosts. This is not my way of asserting that each loss has been replaced by a commensurate gain. This is not an endorsement of bloodletting. But as I moved through these changes, something unexpected happened. As parts of my life grew smaller, other parts expanded. Now, I lean on my own strength. Now, I am my own head and heart. Some days, I still join him in the shower, so I can make sure he doesn't fall. *I don't deserve you*, he says, kissing my forehead. *Try harder*, I suggest, and we laugh.

PRACTICE
(death rattle #6)

The worst part is the dread. For decades,
he was too busy to think about it. Too distracted
to feel it. Death was an abstraction, and then
one day it wasn't. Was it the broken hip? Which
test result? A forgotten name? He can't remember
what caused him to first admit his fragility. But suddenly,
he could see he was a baby bird fallen from a nest.
A chickadee no bigger than a thumb. Eyes closed.
Naked, except for downy gray patches useless
against the weather. Once, he read in a men's magazine
that a person could wake up one day and discover
he'd forgotten how to jump. Experts recommended
daily practice. The upward explosion. The feeling
of your own two feet leaving the earth. He never did it and now
it's true. He can't jump. He's stuck in this chair, death
crouching nearby. He tries to practice what it feels like
to be something on its way to becoming something else.
Like the carcass of a toad, worms threaded through its belly
like shoelaces. Each day, he visualizes melting away.
He's gotten pretty good at it. The most important thing
about jumping, he'd read, was knowing how to land.
Tomorrow, he will practice what it feels like to be
nothing. Like an open window the breeze blows through.

TREASURES

This grief feels too ornate for everyday use.
I wouldn't scrub toilets in fur stole and pearls.
Grief can't sort your pills or change your sheets
or explain for the fifth time it is Thursday today.
I pack it away, and it tarnishes in the darkness
of a dusty upper shelf. Each day, I parade
my administrative genius, and fail to show you
ordinary patience. I don't have time to shine
my lovingkindness. Where can I find
the opulence of time?

Tonight, I choose to share my treasures.
Affix gold hummingbird pin to that red velvet dress.
Set out the wedding china. Light a dozen
beeswax candles that melt into ribbons as we eat
our rice and beans. *Is it my birthday?* you ask.
No, sweetheart, I say. *I'm just happy we're together.*
We tell each other secrets only I will remember,
and I let the dirty dishes crust over because
we need to hold hands on the couch right now,
and watch another rerun of Antiques Roadshow.

AT THE APPOINTED TIME

They spend evenings here now, staring
straight ahead, as if on a routine commute.
He clicks a button. She considers her knitting.
The needles poke out from a fat ball
of wool. They hang in the air like two arrows
protruding from a chest wound.
The remote-control slips, hitting the rug,
as it does every night. And the crinkling
begins, like a cellophane wrapper
from a sexy box of chocolates—or maybe
a bouquet—squeezed and slowly moving
between two palms. Is it coming
from outside? Or within? She pulls back
the curtain. No sign, no light.

It's almost time, she says to her reflection.

EVERY DAY I GET CLOSER TO KNOWING HOW TO SAY GOODBYE

Ordinary days hold most of the clues. Like the days
we laugh when the dog barks at dogs on TV—
or at any animal, really. Even cartoon turkeys. Even a drag queen,
once, decked out in silver feathers. Or the days we reminisce
about moments no one else remembers, like that birthday dinner
for B—you & me, cheering on poor, neurotic P, as he nervously
served the meal. *I like the potatoes, P. I like the salad*—& B,
deadpan, *I like the angst.* And, yes, the days we don't talk at all
because of anger or exhaustion or because the words I use—
garbage day, 401K—belong to a language you no longer speak.
More & more, you drift away. *What is it you see?*
I call to you through an empty soup can, like we're playing
a game of Telephone. *It's just the tea-stained night,* I say,
and we're white handkerchiefs steeping in it, right?
The can still smells like chicken & noodles. I hold it
to my ear. I focus on the hum of the ocean.

SHOEHORNED
(after Elizabeth Alexander)

Among the last things you touched
was your long-handled shoehorn
made of rigid plastic, curved,
navy blue, a practical tool to help you
stay independent. You'd tired
of me, kneeling before you, coaxing
your heels into sturdy slip-on loafers,
adjusting your socks, while you looked away.

Your other shoes were gone: the steel-toed
work boots, the oxblood leather oxfords, the high-top
sneakers with their ladders of laces, the flip flops,
the hip boots, even the slippers
with their fuzzy sheepskin linings, your half
of the matching pairs we got that year
for Christmas, all of that, let go—replaced

by the shoehorn, which I find on the bed,
lying by my pillow, left there after
you slipped on your shoes, then
picked up the pills, carefully placed
your wallet on the dresser, emptied
your pockets, emptied out

the pocket watch, the pearl-
handled penknife, carefully,
the change. You are gone.

THE WIDOW SIFTS THROUGH THE RUBBLE

Any time I had a free hour, I'd drop down
to the basement, try to sort what I wanted
from what I did not. Pulling stuff from closets
and drawers and cobwebbed boxes seemed
to create more stuff: tall teetering piles
labeled with intended destinations.
Goodwill. Garage sale. Jan & Pat.
Stuff overflowed into the crevices
of my life, plugging up my time.

You know what I mean. You stare
at these things from another life,
still yours: yearbooks and diplomas.
Vacation photos. Lace hankies
from dead aunties. Treasure maps
from your past, blocking your future.
How did you get here? You search
the piles for clues, find them
in the florid penmanship of 3rd grade
teachers (*Student shows promise
but needs to be more assertive*),
in the digits of phone numbers
scrawled on cardboard coasters,
in the marriage license signed
by obliging strangers on a golden
fall day on Mt. Hood. Your beloved
world is outdated, frayed, and faded.
Parts of it smell musty. You find
your mind is a half-filled sack containing
old receipts from Home Depot, two family
Bibles (yours and his), endless coils
of electrical cords, uncirculated
coins from the U.S. Mint. I tried
to remember the life I led, the one
that required a pink pageboy wig,
white leather boots, and gossamer wings.

I tried to remember how he shined
his shoes on Sunday nights, buffed them
with the horsehair brush sitting heavy
in my hands. Over & over,
I sifted through old papers—birthday
cards, car titles, sheet music, love
letters. The piles shifted
and bulged like tectonic plates.

My sister helped sometimes, tossing
his woodworking magazines and
muddy running shoes into the trash.
There, they spooned with eyeglass cases,
broken kites, half-used bottles
of hotel shampoo. Within an hour,
she'd exhume bare floor, cutting off
my protests about social need
and landfills. (*Poor people don't want
this shit either, honey.*)

I'd begin again in earnest. Another roll
of blue masking tape. Another set
of garbage bags and boxes. Reaching
through dust to more dust. Excavating
the hardest things: the yellowed
wedding dress, the piece of copper
stove pipe with fluted cap and perfect
green patina that he began to fashion
into a birdhouse for me. The walnut
cane he carved himself, the heart-
shaped pillow from the ICU,
compression socks nested
in an unopened package. Just yesterday,
it seemed, he stocked his cigar box
with sacred objects—feathers
and shells we picked up at Hug Point,

the soft lock of hair he snipped
from my head. I looked for meaning
in all that stuff. But none emerged—
unless you count the postcard I found
and kept: Mount St. Helens, before
the explosion. Shimmering water.
Wildflower meadows. And all along,
the magma below, seeking cracks.

With Thanks

Many thanks are due to many people, especially:

… The Writers Studio, where I've found a creative home—especially school founder and my teacher, Philip Schultz; my Master Class colleagues; and my students, who teach me as much as I teach them. Without all of you, I'd still be roaming around, looking for a narrator.

… my weekly writing group, The Fly Bys, and Write Around Portland, whose community workshops brought The Fly Bys together. Happy 10th Anniversary, Flys!

… Alison Goldstein, Jessica Guernsey, Susan Montgomery, and Rob Sassor, for providing keen feedback and enthusiasm for an early version of this work, as well as unflagging support for all versions of the writer.

LINDA DRACH received her Master in Public Health degree from the University of Michigan and has enjoyed a long career in community health; she currently works as a public health policy manager. She writes poetry, short fiction, and essays; volunteers as a facilitator for community writing workshops with the nonprofit, Write Around Portland; and teaches creative writing at The Writers Studio.

Her poetry and prose have been published in *Bellingham Review, CALYX, Crab Creek Review, The Good Life Review, Lunch Ticket, Okay Donkey*, and elsewhere. She has deep attachments to the Industrial Midwest and the Pacific Northwest, and is a longtime resident of Oregon, where you might find her gardening, kayaking, drinking coffee, or plucking Doug Fir cones from her gutters. Visit her online at lindadrach.com and on Instagram: *@inky_lyrics*.